Paleo Soup
50 Delicious Ca... Friendly Soups

By
Trevor Dumbleton

Liebe!

Wooop Wooop

Soooup time in a Real MaN way

———> caveMaN =)

Happy Times by Trying Soooome MaN soups ...

lots of Love India

2016

Copyright Info
Copyright 2013 Trevor Dumbleton
Stonham House Publishing Company

Paperback Edition

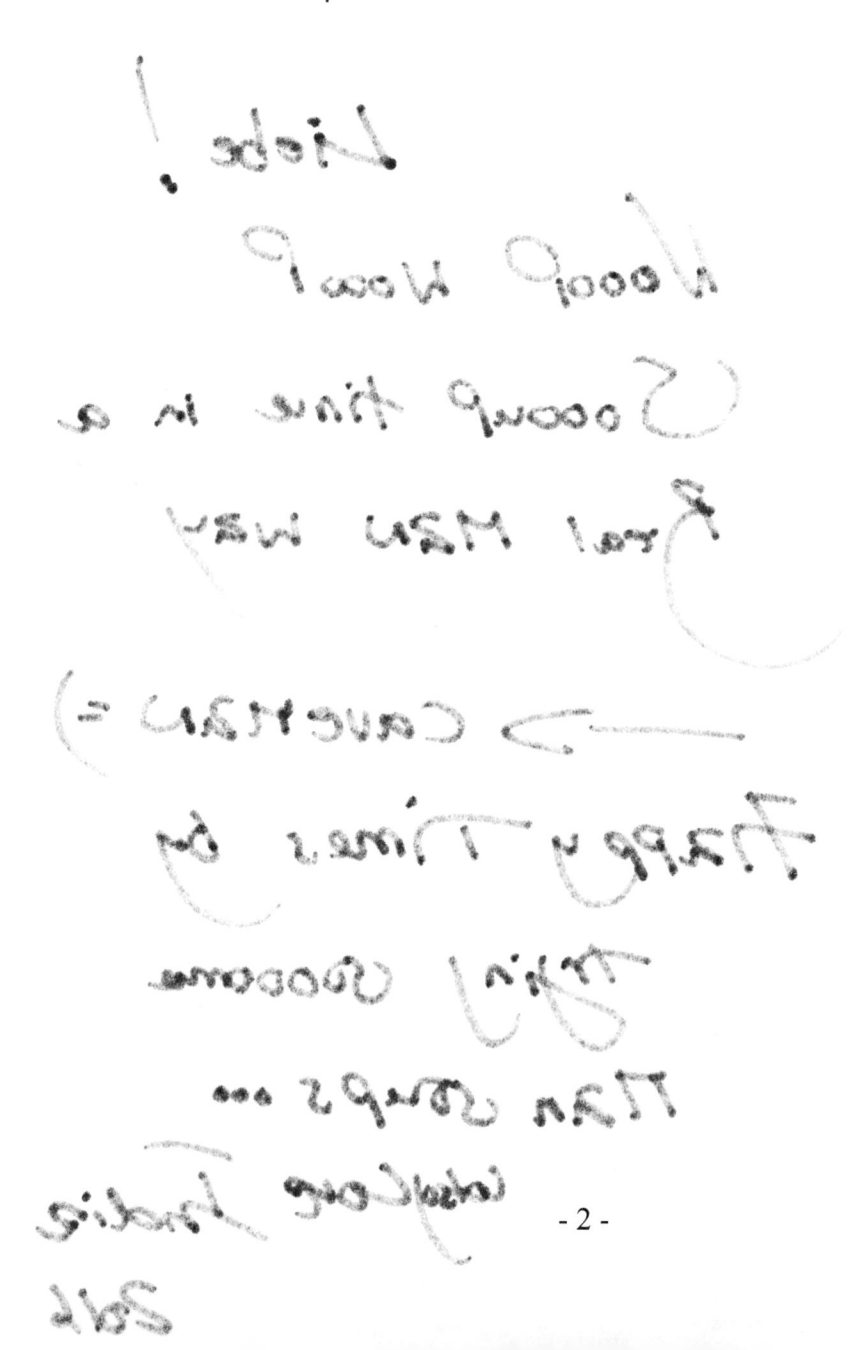

Table of Contents

Artichoke Soup 5
Asparagus Soup 6
Beef & Mushroom Soup 7
Borscht 8
Broccoli and Pine-Nut Soup 9
Broccoli Soup 10
Butternut Squash Soup 11
Cabbage Soup 12
Carrot and Leek Soup 13
Cauliflower Soup 14
Celery Soup 15
Chicken Soup 16
Chicken & Vegetable Soup 18
Chilled Avocado Soup 19
Chilled Creamy Red Pepper Soup 20
Chilled Cucumber Soup 21
Chilled Mango Soup 22
Cock-a-Leekie Soup 23
Cream of Cauliflower Soup 25
Cream of Mushroom Soup 26
Cream of Parsnip Soup 28
Curried Carrot Soup 29
Curried Cauliflower Soup 30
Egg Drop Soup 31
French Onion Soup 33
Gazpacho 35
Hazelnut Soup 36
Hot & Sour Soup 37
Kale Soup 39
Kjotsupa (Icelandic Lamb Soup) 40
Leek and Asparagus Soup 41
Leek and Butternut Squash Soup 42

Leek, Fennel, and Broccoli Soup 43
Minestrone 44
Mulligatawny Soup 45
Pumpkin & Carrot Soup 47
Seafood Soup 49
Slow Roasted Tomato and Fennel Soup 51
Spicy Tomato Soup 53
Spinach and Asparagus Soup 54
Sweet Potato & Lime Soup 55
Tomato & Roasted Red Pepper Soup 57
Tomato and Garlic Soup 58
Turkey Soup 59
Turkey Taco Soup 61
Vegetable Soup 62
Vegetable Soup with Celeriac 63
Watercress Soup 65
Zucchini Summer Soup 67
Zucchini, Scallion and Chive Soup 68

Artichoke Soup
Serves 2-4

Ingredients

2 tablespoons oil
1 yellow onion, chopped
3 garlic cloves, chopped
2 teaspoon ground cumin
28 ounces artichoke hearts
4 cups chicken stock
1 cup water
2 teaspoon fresh mint, chopped
Seasoning to taste

Method

Heat the oil in a pan and sautee the onion for 5 minutes. Add the garlic and sautee for another 2 minutes.

Add the artichoke, cumin, stock and water and bring the mixture to the boil.

Reduce the heat, cover and simmer for 10 minutes.

Puree with a hand blender or liquidizer.

Stir in the mint and season to taste before serving.

Asparagus Soup

Serves 4

Ingredients

2 lbs fresh asparagus, ends removed, chopped into 1-2 inch pieces
1 onion, chopped
3 cloves garlic, minced
1 quart chicken broth
1 tablespoon oil
Seasoning to taste

Method

Sautee the onion and garlic in the oil for about 5 minutes and then add the asparagus, stock and seasoning.

Bring the mixture to the boil and simmer gently for about 5 - 7 minutes until the asparagus becomes tender.

Puree with a hand blender or liquidizer before serving.

Beef & Mushroom Soup

Serves 8

Ingredients

2 pounds ground beef
1 small onion, peeled and chopped
2 tablespoons oil
1 clove garlic, pressed
16 ounces fresh mushrooms, sliced
1 can pumpkin
2 cups beef stock
2 cups chicken stock
Stock cube or beef bouillon granules
Half a cup water
Seasoning to taste

Method

Heat the oil in a large pan. Add the onions, ground beef and garlic. Keep stirring until the beef is sealed and the onions start to soften.

Skim off any excess fat.

Add the remaining ingredients and bring to the boil, stirring as necessary.

Simmer for around 30 - 45 minutes, stirring occasionally.

Borscht

Serves 4

Ingredients

4 cups stock
1 large onion, peeled and chopped
2 large beets, peeled and finely diced
2 carrots, peeled and diced
1 cup thinly sliced or shredded cabbage
Some fresh dill
1 teaspoon lemon juice
Seasoning to taste

Method

Bring the stock, beets, carrots and onion to the boil in a large pan. Once the mixture has come to the boil, add the shredded cabbage. Season with salt & pepper.

Simmer for about 15 minutes.

Add the lemon juice and serve.

Broccoli and Pine-Nut Soup

Serves 4-6

Ingredients

1 onion, peeled and diced
1 tablespoon oil
3 cups broccoli
3 cups chicken or vegetable stock
1/4 cup pine nuts

Method

Heat the oil in a pan and fry the onion until it turns a light brown color.

Add the broccoli and stock, bring to the boil and simmer for around 10 - 15 minutes until the broccoli softens.

Add the pine nuts and then blend until smooth (reserve some pine nuts for garnish if you want).

Re-heat if necessary and serve.

Broccoli Soup

Serves 4

Ingredients

10 ounces frozen chopped broccoli
1/2 cup chopped onions
1 1/3 cup chicken broth
1/2 teaspoon basil, crumbled
1/8 teaspoon white pepper
Sliced almonds

Method

Combine the broccoli, onions and broth in a large pan.

Bring the contents to the boil and simmer gently for 5 minutes.

Blend until smooth using a hand blender.

Add the basil and white pepper and bring the mixture back to barely boiling point.

Simmer for another minute and then serve immediately, sprinkling the almonds on top of each bowl.

Butternut Squash Soup

Serves 6-8

Ingredients

2 lb butternut squash, peeled and cut into chunks
2 tablespoons olive oil
4 cups chicken stock or broth
1/2 teaspoon onion powder
1 teaspoon cayenne or to taste
Seasoning

Method

Put the squash and the stock in a large pan and bring to the boil. Reduce the heat and simmer for 20 minutes until the squash is tender.

Puree the soup with a hand blender.

Stir in the onion powder and other seasoning. Simmer for a further 5 minutes before serving.

Cabbage Soup

Serves 4-6

Ingredients

2 cups beef broth
3/4 medium head cabbage, chopped
2 white onions, chopped
1 green pepper, seeded and chopped
1 mild pepperoncini, finely chopped
1/2 cup chopped celery
4 cups water
2 cans chopped tomatoes
1 clove garlic, chopped
Tabasco sauce (optional)

Method

Place the broth, cabbage, onions, peppers, celery and water in a large pan.

Bring to the boil and then reduce the heat to a gentle simmer.

Add the garlic and Tabasco.

Simmer for around 1 1/2 hours until the vegetables are tender.

Stir in the chopped tomatoes and simmer for another 5 - 10 minutes.

Carrot and Leek Soup
Serves 2-4

Ingredients

1 medium sized leek, finely sliced
5 carrots, diced
1 tablespoon oil
1 tablespoon ground ginger
3 cups vegetable stock

Method

Place a pan on a medium heat, add the oil and then add the leek and carrots and sautee them until they become tender.

Add vegetable stock, bring to the boil and simmer for 10-15 minutes.

Remove from heat and serve.

Cauliflower Soup

Serves 6-8

Ingredients

4 tablespoons oil
4 tablespoons arrowroot
10 cups stock
1 whole cauliflower, chopped
Handful parsley, freshly chopped

Method

Heat the oil in a large pan and make a roux by adding the arrowroot. Stir the mixture continuously for 1 minute.

Add the vegetable stock slowly to stop lumps forming, stirring as you add the stock.

Add the cauliflower into the pan, bring the mixture to the boil and simmer it for another 20-30 minutes.

Mash the cauliflower in the pan (or use a hand blender).

Add the freshly chopped parsley and cook for another 5 minutes.

Serve.

Celery Soup

Serves 2-4

Ingredients

1 1/2 bunches celery
2 cups water
1 to 2 tablespoons flax seeds
1/2 lemon, juiced
1 garlic clove, minced
1 jalapeno, diced
1 red pepper, seeded and finely chopped
1 soft avocado, pitted and sliced
Seasoning to taste

Method

Place all the ingredients in a pan and bring the mixture to the boil.

Reduce the heat and simmer for about 15-20 minutes until the celery is soft.

Blend all the ingredients with a hand blender or liquidizer and serve.

Chicken Soup

Serves 4-6

Ingredients

6 boneless skinless chicken thighs
6 cups chicken broth
1 can of diced tomatoes
2 carrots, chopped
1/2 a large onion, diced finely
1 teaspoon crushed garlic
2 big handfuls of spinach
Dried thyme
Dried oregano
Seasoning
1 Tablespoons oil

Method

Heat the oil in a large pan and add the onions, garlic and carrots. Cook them for about 5 minutes until they start to become tender.

Add the chicken, tomatoes, stock and seasoning.

Bring to the boil and simmer for about 20 minutes - make sure the chicken is cooked right through.

Take the chicken out and shred it. Place the shredded chicken back in the pan.

Stir in the spinach and simmer for another 10 minutes.

Serve immediately.

Chicken & Vegetable Soup

Serves 5-6

Ingredients

6 cups water or stock
4 chicken portions, diced
2 gloves garlic, minced
1 medium onion, peeled and diced
1 bay leaf
1 teaspoon black pepper
6 tomatoes, diced
2 small zucchini, thinly sliced
3 carrots, diced

Method

Put the water or stock, chicken, garlic, onion, bay leaf and pepper in a large pan and bring it to the boil.

Cover and simmer gently for about an hour.

Remove the bay leaf and add the other ingredients.

Bring the soup back to the boil and simmer for about 20 minutes until the carrots are tender.

Chilled Avocado Soup

Serves 4-6

Ingredients

2-3 large, peeled and diced avocados
1 cup water
Juice from 1 to 2 limes
1/4 cup chopped green onions
1/4 cup chopped fresh cilantro
2 minced serrano chilli
2 cloves garlic, minced
1 teaspoon chili powder
6 tablespoons chopped fresh mint leaves
3 cups chicken broth
Seasoning to taste

Method

Combine all the ingredients except the broth and seasoning in a blender until smooth.

Transfer the mixture to a large bowl and gradually whisk in the broth.

Season to taste and then place in a refrigerator for at least 2 hours until the soup is cold.

Chilled Creamy Red Pepper Soup

Serves 2

Ingredients

2 roasted red bell peppers, seeded and roughly chopped
1 14-ounce can coconut milk
1 cup chilled chicken stock
1 teaspoon cumin
Seasoning to taste

Method

Place the roasted peppers in a blender with the coconut milk, stock and cumin.

Blend the mixture until smooth.

Place in a bowl, add seasoning, cover and place in a refrigerator for at least 2 hours before serving.

Chilled Cucumber Soup

Serves 2-4

Ingredients

2 medium cucumbers, peeled and chopped
1/2 cup chopped onion
1/4 cup fresh cilantro leaves
1/2 cup coconut milk
1/4 cup chicken broth

Method

Place all the ingredients into a blender and blend until smooth.

Place the soup in a refrigerator for at least 4 hours before serving.

Chilled Mango Soup

Serves 8

Ingredients

8 large ripe mangoes, pitted, peeled and diced
4 Valencia oranges
2 (14 oz.) cans coconut milk
2 limes
4 ounces fresh ginger, peeled and cut into 1/2 inch chunks
1 small bunch Thai basil (optional), stems removed, finely chopped
1 small bunch cilantro, stems removed, finely chopped
1 tablespoons oil

Method

As this is a chilled soup, put the cans of coconut milk in the refrigerator for at least 2 hours before making this recipe.

Zest the limes using a grater.

Cut the limes and oranges in half and squeeze the juice out of them into a large bowl.

Place the ginger and about two thirds of the mangoes in a food processor together with the coconut milk. Blend until these have mixed together.

Cock-a-Leekie Soup

Serves 4-6

Ingredients

2 tablespoons oil
1lb chicken portions
2 large leeks (sliced lengthways then cut into approximately 1/2 inch half moons)
2 or 3 bacon rashers, chopped (optional)
4 pints chicken stock
Bouquet garni
Seasoning to taste
8 prunes, stoned and halved
Parsley sprigs to garnish

Method

Heat the oil in a pan and fry the chicken on all sides until it is a light golden brown color.

Add the leeks and - if you're using it - the bacon. Sautee for about 5 minutes.

Add the stock, bouquet garni and seasoning.

Bring the mixture to the boil, reduce the heat, cover and simmer for about an hour.

Add the prunes and simmer for another half an hour.

Remove the chicken and chop it into pieces.

Place the chicken in bowls and pour the soup over the top, garnishing with the parsley.

Cream of Cauliflower Soup

Serves 2-4

Ingredients

1 large head of cauliflower, diced
2 - 3 stalks celery, chopped
1 carrot, diced
2 cloves garlic
2 onions, peeled and chopped
1 teaspoon ground cumin
1/2 teaspoon pepper
1/4 teaspoon sage
A few sprigs of parsley

Method

Place the cauliflower, celery, carrot, onion, garlic and spices in a large pan.

Top up the pan with water or stock until the ingredients are barely covered.

Bring to the boil and simmer for about 20 minutes until the vegetables are tender.

Blend the soup to a creamy consistency and serve.

Cream of Mushroom Soup
Serves 2

Ingredients

1 avocado, peeled and pitted
2 tomatoes, diced
1 cup hot water
1 red sweet pepper, seeded and diced
1 tablespoon oil
1 cup mushrooms, sliced
1 red sweet pepper, diced
1 small onion, peeled and diced
1 clove of garlic, minced
Juice of 1/2 grapefruit
Chopped basil

Method

Blend the avocado, grapefruit juice, garlic and hot water in a food processor.

Heat the oil in a large pan and sautee the mushrooms, pepper, onion, tomato and basil until they start to soften.

Stir in the avocado mixture and bring to the boil.

Simmer for 5 minutes or so until the mushrooms are tender.

If you like a smoother soup, use a hand blender before serving.

Cream of Parsnip Soup
Serves 4

Ingredients

1lb parsnips, peeled and diced.
1 onion, peeled and chopped
4 cups stock or water
Seasoning to taste
2 tablespoons coconut milk

Method

Place the parsnips, onion, stock and seasoning in a large pan and bring to the boil.

Cover and simmer for 20 - 30 minutes until the parsnips are tender.

Blend the soup with a hand blender.

Stir in the coconut milk immediately before serving.

Curried Carrot Soup

Serves 5-6

Ingredients

1 tablespoon curry powder
1/2 teaspoon ground black pepper
A pinch of cayenne pepper
A pinch of ground ginger
1 tablespoon oil
1 large onion, peeled and chopped
2 cloves garlic, minced
2 lbs carrots, washed, peeled and chopped
3 cups vegetable stock
1 can coconut milk
Fresh parsley, for garnish

Method

Heat the oil in a large pan and saute the onion and garlic until they soften.

Stir in the spices and then add the carrots and stock (add more water if the vegetables aren't covered completely).

Bring to the boil, cover and simmer for about 30 minutes until the carrots become tender.

Use a hand blender to puree the soup, then gently stir in the coconut milk.

Serve immediately, garnished with parsley.

Curried Cauliflower Soup

Serves 4-6

Ingredients

1 tablespoon oil
1 diced onion
1 finely chopped garlic clove
1 teaspoon ground cumin
1 teaspoon ground turmeric
1 tablespoon ground coriander
1 tablespoon ground paprika
1/2 medium cauliflower
4 cups vegetable stock
Seasoning to taste

Method

Fry the diced onion and garlic in a little oil over a medium heat until they turn light brown in color.

Add the cauliflower, turmeric, coriander, cumin. Continue to heat the mixture, stirring continuously for 2 minutes.

Add the vegetable stock, bring to the boil, then cover the pan and simmer for 10-20 minutes.

Remove from the heat and serve.

Egg Drop Soup
Serves 4

Ingredients

4 cups (just over 1.5 pints) chicken stock
A pinch of ground or dried ginger
2 tablespoons chopped scallions (also known as spring onions)
A pinch of salt (optional)
4 eggs, beaten

Method

Put all the ingredients except the eggs in a large pan and bring to the boil.

Simmer for a few minutes so that the scallions soften.

Remove the scallions if you want to (you can use them as a garnish later) or leave them in the soup if you prefer it that way.

Stir the soup - some say clockwise is best - and slowly pour in the beaten egg.

Resist the temptation to stir whilst the eggs cook - this will take about a minute.

Because we haven't thickened the soup with corn flour, the eggs won't be quite the same as you'll get in a restaurant - they'll puff up rather than cook in ribbons - but they'll still taste nice.

Serve immediately.

French Onion Soup

Serves 6-8

Ingredients

6 large onions, peeled and sliced. Don't cut them too small
2 tablespoons oil
2 cloves garlic, crushed
8 cups stock
Fresh or dried thyme
Bay leaf
Seasoning to taste

Method

Heat the oil in a large saucepan. Add the onions, stirring occasionally, until they've turned brown. Make sure that they don't burn in the process - if you've got a thick bottomed pan that will help.

Once the onions are nicely brown, stir in the garlic and heat it through.

Then add the stock or a mix of stock and water.

Add in the thyme and the bay leaf.

Bring to the boil and simmer for about half an hour.

Add salt and pepper to taste.

Remove the bay leaf.

Gazpacho

Serves 8

Ingredients

2 cups peeled and diced cucumber
2 cups diced red bell pepper
2 cups diced ripe tomato
1/2 cup diced red onion
2 cups tomato juice
1/2 cup lemon juice
1/3 cup extra-virgin olive oil
Tabasco sauce
Seasoning to taste

Method

Place the cucumber, pepper, tomato and onion into a large bowl.

Add in the tomato juice, lemon juice, oil, seasoning and Tabasco.

Mix together well.

Blend to your desired consistency.

Cover and refrigerate for at least 6 hours or ideally overnight.

Hazelnut Soup

Serves 4-6

Ingredients

2 cups ground unroasted hazelnuts
4 cups beef or chicken broth
1 medium onion, peeled and diced
1 1/2 Tablespoons chopped parsley
Seasoning to taste

Method

Place all the ingredients in a large pan and bring it to the boil.

Reduce the heat and simmer gently for about an hour, stirring occasionally.

Serve immediately.

Hot & Sour Soup

Serves 4

Ingredients

1 cup sliced mushrooms
1 can of bamboo shoots
3 tablespoons apple vinegar cider
1 1/2 tablespoons fish sauce
1 tablespoon arrowroot
4 cups chicken broth
2 eggs, beaten
1 teaspoon sesame oil
Seasoning to taste
3 scallions, diced (optional)
1/4 teaspoon of chili oil (optional)

Method

Place the mushrooms in a strainer and put a pan or similar below the strainer. Pour 1 1/2 cups of boiling water over the mushrooms.

Mix the mushroom water with the arrowroot to form a thin paste.

Mix the cider vinegar and fish sauce together and set them aside.

Drain the bamboo shoots and slice them into long strips.

Bring the stock to the boil in a large pan and then add the mushrooms, bamboo shoots, vinegar & fish sauce mixture and arrowroot paste.

Stir continuously whilst it comes back to the boil.

Remove the soup from the heat and slowly stir in the beaten egg.

If you are using scallions, add them now. Also add the seasoning and sesame oil.

Serve immediately.

Kale Soup

Serves 6

Ingredients

3 leeks, chopped
1 bunch kale cleaned, drained and chopped
1 cup sliced mushrooms with stems
2 onions, peeled and chopped
4 celery stalks, cut horizontally
1 zucchini, chopped
1 pound baby carrots, peeled
4-5 fresh tomatoes, chopped
2 tablespoons oil
4 pints chicken stock
1 teaspoon thyme
5 basil leaves
3 garlic cloves, crushed
Seasoning to taste

Method

Heat the oil in a pan and sautee the vegetables in it for about 10 minutes until they start to become tender.

Add the stock, herbs and seasoning.

Bring the mixture to the boil, cover and gently simmer for an hour.

Kjotsupa (Icelandic Lamb Soup)

Serves 6-8

Ingredients

6 pints water
2lb lamb, cut into large pieces
1 red onion, peeled and sliced
2 medium carrots, peeled and diced
1lb rutabaga, peeled and diced
1/2lb sweet potatoes, peeled and diced
1 leek

Method

Bring the water to the boil and add the meat. Reduce the heat to a gentle simmer and cook for about 40 minutes.

Add the remaining ingredients and any seasoning, bring back to the boil and simmer for another 20 minutes.

Serve piping hot.

Leek and Asparagus Soup

Serves 2-4

Ingredients

8 asparagus spears, chopped into 1 inch pieces
2 tablespoons oil
1 1/2 cups leek, sliced
1 garlic clove, finely chopped
1 1/2 cups stock
1/2 cup coconut milk
Seasoning

Method

Sautee the leek and garlic in the oil for about 5 minutes or until leek has softened.

Now add the asparagus and stock to the pan, bring it to the boil and simmer gently for another 15 minutes or until asparagus has softened.

Remove from heat and add coconut milk.

Leave it for 5-10 minutes openly.

Puree with a hand blender or liquidizer.

Add seasoning and serve.

Leek and Butternut Squash Soup

Serves 4

Ingredients

4 leeks, trimmed and diced
6 ounces butternut squash (peeled weight)
1 large onion, peeled and chopped
1 tablespoons oil
2 pints stock
1 clove garlic, crushed
Seasoning to taste

Method

Heat the oil in a pan and add the vegetables, stirring well. On a low heat, allow the vegetables to sweat for around 20 minutes, stirring occasionally.

Add the stock and seasoning and bring to the boil. Cover the pan and simmer for 20 minutes.

Blend with a hand blender or liquidizer before serving.

Leek, Fennel, and Broccoli Soup

Serves 2-4

Ingredients

2 garlic cloves, finely chopped
1 tablespoon olive oil
1 sliced leek
1 large fennel, stalks removed and diced
1 chopped broccoli
4 cups vegetable stock
2 bay leaves
1/2 cup coconut milk

Method

Sautee the chopped garlic, leek and fennel in oil in a large pan over a medium heat for 5-8 minutes until they become tender.

Add broccoli, bay leaves and vegetable stock.

Bring to the boil and then cover the pan and simmer for 10 minutes.

Remove it from heat.

Add the coconut milk.

Optionally, puree the soup with a hand blender.

Minestrone

Serves 2-4

Ingredients

1 tablespoon of olive oil
1 carrot, sliced
1/4 medium onion, chopped
1 teaspoon garlic
1 can chopped tomatoes
2 cups stock
1 teaspoon Italian seasoning
1 small zucchini, chopped
2 handfuls spinach

Method

Saute the onions, carrot and garlic in the oil for about 5 minutes until they are soft.

Add the tomatoes, stock and seasoning.

Bring to the boil and simmer for about 20 minutes.

Add the zucchini and spinach, bring back to the boil and simmer for another 10 minutes.

Mulligatawny Soup

Serves 4-6

Ingredients

2 tablespoons oil
1/3 cup onions, finely diced
1/3 cup red bell peppers, seeded and finely diced
1 cup peeled apples, diced
2 carrots, diced
2 sticks celery, diced
1 tablespoon curry powder
4 cups chicken or lamb stock
3/4 cup coconut milk
1 tablespoon kuzu root starch or arrowroot
1/3 lb diced lamb
1 tablespoon lemon juice
1/4 teaspoon salt
1/8 teaspoon ground red pepper
1/8 teaspoon thyme
1 tablespoon chopped fresh cilantro

Method

Mix the root starch or arrowroot with 3 tablespoons of cold water. Stir this into the coconut milk and set aside.

Saute the lamb in some oil until it is brown. Set aside.

Saute the onions and the peppers in some oil until soft, 2 - 3 minutes depending on how finely you've diced them.

Add in the carrots and celery and saute for another 3 minutes.

Add the curry powder and saute for another 2 minutes, stirring continuously.

Add the stock, lamb and apples.

Bring the mixture to the boil and simmer for around 20 minutes. Don't cover the pan.

Stir in the coconut milk mixture and other ingredients (except the cilantro) and simmer for 5 minutes.

Add the cilantro and serve immediately.

Pumpkin & Carrot Soup

Serves 4-6

Ingredients

Half a small sized pumpkin, peeled, seeded and cut into large chunks
4 large carrots, peeled and cut into large chunks
1 large onion, peeled and chopped
1 cup chicken stock
1 clove garlic
1 sprig chervil, chopped
Several parsley leaves, chopped
Several coriander leaves, chopped
3 tablespoons of oil

Method

Heat the oil in a large pan and sautee the onion until it turns slightly golden in color.

Add the garlic, carrot and pumpkin. Add some water to part-cover the ingredients but don't use too much as the carrots and pumpkin will reduce in size as they cook.

Bring the mixture to the boil and add the parsley, chervil and coriander.

Reduce the heat, cover and simmer for around 25 minutes until the carrots are cooked.

Add the chicken stock and bring back to a gentle simmer for about 5 minutes.

Blend the soup to produce a creamy texture.

Seafood Soup

Serves 4-6

Ingredients

2 cups coconut milk
1 small onion, peeled and thinly sliced
1 medium red bell pepper, seeded and cut into thin strips
2 pounds red snapper fillets, sea bass, or similar, cut into 2 inch pieces
1 pound medium shrimp, peeled, rinsed and de-veined
1 tablespoon coconut oil
1 teaspoon dried oregano
1/4 teaspoon annatto (optional)
Freshly ground black pepper
1 medium banana, peeled and cut into 1 inch slices
1 medium tomato, diced
3 tablespoons minced cilantro leaves

Method

Sautee the onion and pepper in the oil for a minute or so until the onion starts to soften.

Add the coconut milk, oregano, annatto and pepper and bring to the boil.

Simmer for 5 minutes before adding the fish and shrimp.

Bring the soup back to the boil and gently simmer for about 10 minutes until the fish is cooked.

Add the banana and tomato to the soup and simmer for 5 minutes.

Stir in the cilantro leaves immediately before serving.

Slow Roasted Tomato and Fennel Soup

Serves 6-8

Ingredients

3 lbs whole fresh tomatoes, cored and halved
1 fennel bulb, stem removed, quartered
1 large yellow onion, peeled and cut into quarters
2 large carrots, peeled and cut in half
2 stalks celery, cut in half
3 cloves garlic, peeled
3 Tablespoons olive oil
6 cups stock
1 teaspoon ground cumin
1 teaspoon smoked paprika
Seasoning to taste

Method

Using 1 tablespoon of the oil, lightly coat the fennel, celery, carrots, onion and garlic. Place them onto a sheet pan.

Toss the tomatoes with the other 2 tablespoons of oil. Place them onto a sheet pan.

Heat the oven to 275 degrees F, 140 degrees C, gas mark 1.

Place both trays in the oven and roast for around 1 hour 45 minutes to 2 hours.

Transfer all the vegetables to a pan and add the stock.

Bring the mixture to the boil and simmer gently until the tomatoes begin to break apart.

Puree with a hand blender or liquidizer.

If you want, strain the soup so that the skins, seeds, etc are removed.

Return the soup to the heat and add the spices and seasoning to taste.

Spicy Tomato Soup

Serves 3-4

Ingredients

8 tomatoes pureed or a can of chopped tomatoes
1 cup water
1/4 cup green chilies, seeded and chopped
1 red onion, peeled and finely chopped
1 clove garlic, minced
1 bell pepper, seeded and chopped
1 teaspoon cayenne pepper
1 teaspoon paprika

Method

Place all the ingredients in a large pan and bring to the boil.

Cover and simmer gently for an hour.

Spinach and Asparagus Soup

Serves 2-4

Ingredients

4 chopped scallions or spring onions
4 cups spinach
6 thick asparagus spears, sliced in half
Vegetable oil
1 can coconut milk
Spices to taste

Method

Fry the chopped scallions in a little oil on medium heat until the scallions turn to a light brown color.

Add all the spices, asparagus and spinach and stir until everything is mixed well.

Lastly, add coconut milk, bring to the boil and simmer the soup for 10-15 minutes.

Sweet Potato & Lime Soup

Serves 4

Ingredients

3 medium sweet potatoes, peeled and cut into chunks
4 cups chicken stock
3 thin slices fresh ginger
2 lime leaves
3/4 cup coconut milk
1/2 cup water
2 tablespoons lime juice
2 tablespoons cilantro, finely chopped
Seasoning to taste

Method

Place the sweet potatoes, stock, ginger and lime leaves in a large pan and bring the contents to the boil.

Reduce the heat and simmer for 20 minutes until the sweet potatoes are tender.

Remove the lime leaves and then blend the soup until it's smooth.

Add the coconut milk, water, lime juice and seasoning and gently bring the mixture back to the boil.

Serve immediately, using the cilantro as garnish.

Tomato & Roasted Red Pepper Soup

Serves 2-4

Ingredients

2 cans crushed tomatoes
1 cup onions, peeled and chopped
1 tablespoons oil
1 cup vegetable or chicken broth
1/2 cup roasted red peppers
1/2 cup fresh basil
3 cloves garlic, chopped

Method

Heat the oil in a skillet and add the onions. Sautee until the onions begin to caramelize and then add the garlic.

In a separate pan, bring the tomatoes and broth to boiling point.

Using a blender, puree the roasted red peppers and the basil. Add this and the onions to the soup base.

Add seasoning as desired.

Simmer gently for about 15 minutes before serving.

Tomato and Garlic Soup
Serves 2

Ingredients

1 can of chopped plum tomatoes
1 large onion, chopped and peeled. Your choice as to whether this is a white or a red onion
1 tablespoon oil
1 clove garlic, crushed
A splash of soy sauce (optional)
A dash of barbecue sauce (optional)
2 teaspoons wholegrain mustard
Seasoning to taste

Method

Heat the oil in a saucepan and fry the onion and garlic until they soften.

Add the rest of the ingredients and bring to the boil.

Simmer for around 8 minutes until the flavors start to fuse together.

Serve as is or blend until smooth.

Turkey Soup

Serves 4-6

Ingredients

1lb diced turkey
4 rashers of turkey bacon, chopped (optional)
1 large onion, peeled and chopped
1 leek, sliced
1 tablespoons oil
1 clove garlic, crushed
4 carrots, peeled and chopped
6 sticks of celery, chopped
A pinch of dried thyme
1 zucchini
1 parsnip, peeled and chopped
1 sweet potato, peeled and chopped
1 teaspoon Worcester sauce
Pepper to taste
1 cup Chicken Broth
1 can of chopped tomatoes

Method

Heat the oil in a pan and saute the onions until they are soft.

Add the thyme, garlic, turkey and turkey bacon and cook for another 2 - 3 minutes.

Add the remaining ingredients, topping up with water if needed.

Bring to the boil, reduce the heat, cover and simmer for 2 hours.

Optionally, blend the soup before serving.

Turkey Taco Soup

Serves 4-6

Ingredients

20 ounces Ground Turkey
1 onion, peeled and chopped
2 Tablespoons chili powder
1 Tablespoons cumin
1 Tablespoons oil
2 cups diced tomatoes
4 cups chicken stock
1/2 cabbage, sliced into strips
1 avocado, peeled, pitted & cubed

Method

Heat the oil in a pan, add the ground turkey and spices and stir until the turkey is browned.

Add the tomatoes, stock and cabbage.

Bring to the boil and simmer gently for an hour before serving with the cubed avocado.

Vegetable Soup

Serves 4-6

Ingredients

1/2 cup diced red onions
1/2 cup diced white onions
1 cup diced tomatoes
1 cup celery, cut into 2 inch sections
1 cup sliced carrots
1 cup sliced zucchini
3 tablespoons diced fresh diced parsley
3 tablespoons diced fresh garlic
3 bay leaves
Seasoning to taste
1 tablespoon olive oil
3 cups water

Method

Heat the oil in a pan and saute all the ingredients (except the water and seasoning) for about 10 minutes until the vegetables start to become tender.

Add the water and bring the mixture to the boil. Add seasoning to taste and simmer for 45 minutes before serving.

Vegetable Soup with Celeriac
Serves 10

Ingredients

2 slices bacon (optional, uncured for preference)
2 tablespoons oil
1 medium onion, peeled and chopped
1 pound mushrooms, chopped
3 stalks celery, chopped
2 cloves garlic, crushed
2 tablespoons tomato paste
1 celeriac, finely diced (it looks ugly but don't let that put you off)
5 cups stock
A few drops of Tabasco sauce
1 teaspoon dried thyme
2 bay leaves
Seasoning to taste

Method

If you're including bacon, fry it until crisp and then set aside so that it cools down.

Fry the onions in either the bacon fat or some oil until they start to soften and turn brown. Add in the mushrooms and sweat them down so that they reduce in size.

Add in the celery and cook for another few minutes.

Add in the garlic and the tomato paste, stirring well to mix them in.

Add in the rest of the ingredients and bring to the boil. Simmer the soup for around 15 minutes so that the celeriac becomes tender.

Adjust the seasoning if needed.

If you're using bacon, chop it into small pieces.

Remove the bay leaves and serve, using the bacon as a garnish.

Watercress Soup

Serves 8-10

Ingredients

1 tablespoons oil
1 onion, peeled and chopped
5 stalks of celery, chopped
1 1/2 cups of radishes, chopped
1 cup cauliflower
2 tablespoons lemon juice
2 tablespoons lemon verbena
2 teaspoon dried coriander
2 teaspoon dried basil
32 ounces chicken stock
1 can coconut milk
6 packed cups watercress leaves and stem
1 tablespoons garlic powder

Method

Heat the oil in a pan and sautee the onion, celery and radishes for a few minutes until they soften.

Stir in the lemon verbena, coriander, basil.

Add the coconut milk and stock, bring to the boil and simmer gently until the radishes are tender.

Add about 4 1/2 cups of watercress, keep simmering until the watercress has wilted.

Add the garlic powder and any other seasoning.

Blend the soup until it is smooth then return to a gentle simmer for about 10 minutes.

Serve with the remaining watercress (chopped) as garnish.

Zucchini Summer Soup

Serves 4-6

Ingredients

2 tablespoons oil
2 1/4 lbs zucchini, chopped
Handful of fresh basil
Handful of fresh parsley, stalks removed
1 pint of water
Seasoning to taste

Method

Sautee the zucchini in the oil for about 10 - 15 minutes, stirring occasionally, until they have shrunk in size.

Add seasoning and water and bring the mixture to the boil.

Remove from the heat and add the basil and parsley.

Blend to a thick and creamy consistency.

Either serve immediately or place in a refrigerator for at least 6 hours if you want to serve this soup chilled.

Zucchini, Scallion and Chive Soup

Serves 4

Ingredients

1/2 cup zucchini, shredded
1/2 cup shallots, chopped
1 clove garlic, minced
1 tablespoons olive oil
1 cup scallions, chopped
1/2 cup chives, chopped
2 cups chicken broth
1/2 cup water

Method

Heat the oil in a pan and add the zucchini, shallots and garlic, stirring regularly, for about 5 minutes until the shallots are tender.

Add the scallions and about half the chives and cook, stirring regularly, for another 2 minutes.

Add the broth and water and bring the mixture to the boil.

Simmer for about 5 minutes before blending the soup to a smooth consistency.

If necessary, re-heat before serving with the remaining chives as garnish.

Printed in Great Britain
by Amazon